The Echo Chamber

To my bestest friend ever.
I love you xx Angela

Matt Chamberlain
& Angela Dye

Whisky
&
Beards

Copyright © 2018 Matt Chamberlain & Angela Dye

All rights reserved.

ISBN-13: 978-1986123358

ISBN-10: 1986123359

Cover image: "Listening From The Gut" by Elizabeth S. Dye, 2018

All rights reserved. No part of this publication may be reproduced, distributed, or transmitted in any form or by any means, including photocopying, recording, or other electronic or mechanical methods, without prior written permission of the publisher, except in the case of brief quotations embodied in critical reviews and certain other non-commercial uses permitted by copyright law.

For permission requests, contact the publisher or author

Whisky & Beards Publishing
WhiskyandBeards.co.uk

CONTENTS

Many Little Midnights	2
Feeling Blue	4
Losing Touch	5
Matters of the Heart	7
Embrace	9
Prose Bush	11
Pop!	14
Soup	15
Clear	19
Two-fold Souls	21
Slacken	26
To Fall: In Love	28
Wolf	31
Dancing with Wolves in My Eyes	33
Then	35
Match	36
Colour-match	40
Auld Lang Syne	41

IN LOVING MEMORY
OF GEORGE CHAMBERLAIN
1942 - 2017

FOREWORD by Connor Sansby

Two poets mulling over project ideas found themselves drawn to David Bowie's early-career method of song-writing. Suppose they too abandoned planning and instead allowed ideas to attack, embrace or bounce off each other? With an opening poem plucked out of the sky, subsequent poems would be stimulated by what went before, but loosely and unevenly so. Concepts would be repeated and themes subverted and, as the book progressed, ideas would repeat and reverberate, layers would develop and perspectives would change and maybe change back. A story might just emerge. It might just go somewhere – or nowhere. In the event, it roamed far but ended up back somewhere close to the place where it had started.

Welcome to The Echo Chamber, where one writer provides beautiful lyrical, anchoring poems and the other flies away with powerful concepts and glides on curious thermals. Steeped in metaphor and mixing reality and unreality, autobiographical and fictional, these forceful-yet-sensitive poems never jostle or compete; they feed each other. Beginning and ending with midnights, the book wakes quietly but clashes and clangs in crescendo. Take your torch into the Chamber; hear the notes; see the colours; taste the brewed berries and observe the many deaths.

You, too, may come full circle.

MANY LITTLE MIDNIGHTS

I don't really know
if they're blueberries, bilberries or sloes
but they grow in the corners of my eyes as I slide
down muddy paths that looked straighter
in the height of summer. They linger, less obvious
than the April blossom, or the hedgerow's summer socks

fashioned from cow parsley lace, looming only
in October when they softly sing plush hymns.

One day we crunched
across fields in time with a rifle crack,
our pickings more plentiful than those
of the faithful gundog, bemused at
his master's rotary machine which lured no pigeons
but attracted our mirth. On we picked. And on
our return we made something we called gin
although we didn't really care
whether the ingredient was blueberries, bilberries or
sloes.

They are hard to describe, being
well towards the darker end of indigo
yet somehow also lax white powder-coated –
blown smoke masking many little midnights.
I wonder whether this is all designed
to get me to look at them more, and,
sidestepping well-stagnated puddles, I do. They look
like jelly babies' faces, swept chalkboards, talcum-
coated squash balls.

If I removed a glove and licked a finger, I could
write my name on them, but inch long javelins keep them
pure. More contained than grasping brambles,
these scythed chariot wheels rumble through
my potholed afternoons. Comforting, familiar,
they seem to matter; though I do not much mind
if they are blueberries, bilberries or sloes.

FEELING BLUE

Is it you I hear again, slick sliding in
with the moon, past midnight – I thought you would
never come. So many blue stained nights I have
waited taut for you to slink into my scathed skin.
The corner of my eye blinks she saw you. No,
it's only my shorn shadow framed in etiolate
rain. Moonshine shimmies slow dancing confetti
down walls. Swift brush silver dust off my dreams,
lick you from my fingers. The way you smiled
once, it is the little things that matter:
the way you would tuck the edge of the bed,
you said you would drown the moon for me.
Is it you I hear this many moons past
many midnights? Broken, maimed, cold, whatever
you are, I do not much mind. Come: be home.

LOSING TOUCH

It's all those little things. Taut tide comes back every day.
It's the not noticing; the complacency. Laps liquid, gentle scuff of whiskered kiss.
It's being taken for granted; the little liberties.
Waves carry micro diamond grinding blades.

You don't notice tiny knives or feel the tiny deaths.

Little on more little. Hear again, unremitting tide.

The selective hearing; the having to think twice. Dogged sea recoups the Isle.

When laughter stops; when everything's a compromise. Rain pats cliff face; nibble now a bite.

You don't notice powdered drift is now crumbled cheese sliding silently off the blade.

It's the losing touch. Little tide; one nip too many.

Those points of no return crossed blindly. Land of plenty
broken, maimed by fairy dust.

The swimming static. Vanish vertical. Land-drop vast
enough to drown the moon.

Having tucked the edge you do not notice phantom
crash and bitemarks given granite. You notice

when it's gone.

MATTERS OF THE HEART

I think I knew it was you,
when I found all those small
scattered things, not the strata
of our skeletons that stretched
tall to climb the cliff face, but
those diamond pixels
of lowered lights, so aware
of poems, strung like nerves to hang a man

between shadowed trees where the sea
bit the earth green, where tired stars wept
from a cold wave and the grave grip
of salt rusted points to blood. When all the wood
was swept up and I saw the footsteps, I saw
those other lost things: a cry, a lie, a spell, the things
that should never have mattered. Many calls
at midnight, I did not think twice about dying

for you. When bed sheets tautly tied loosen
and the continental drifts across oceans too
vast to clamour over: the lies, crystallised lies
lie between hammered lands and chiselled trust.
How many bespoke drops does it take to make
the ocean drown and choke, choke, choke
on grinding salt?   Pass.
There are two monsters preserved in the cliff

faces, where sandy kisses or just one storm swill
will erode and loosen them. Why does a man feel
alienation and loss when all he did is love…oh
life lives at the fine edge of things. In a split
second we fall one side of a silver blade or

the other: in slivers of spliced time, creamy flesh
is laid to waste. Is a man the scum of his spilt
thoughts, a gathering of frayed fragments, the sod

of small things-the purple of his heart wrapped
in thorns, powdered with morals or mischief?
When I called you, many midnights passed,
I don't think you were able to garner my rubies,
my broken pearls let loose on the stone
threshing floor. These are my memories, bits
of you that I want to lose. Sharp cut, sawn
from dawn moorings to set sail past a clutch

of red heart broken sunsets, wine washed
spirits at the helm. Now please touch my
head on soil, a place to make my bed
in a field that is half ploughed. The autumn sun
kissing whiskery ears of corn you will grind
to break my mourning bread, where I will
not even remember what taste you were.
And I think, does anything matter anymore?

EMBRACE

The size and hue of a frayed Penny Black, St James's contains
universes. Somehow bright inside, narrow lancet windows
heave in sunlight like golden rope
yet, outside, only clouds the colour of gruel emboss
the great wash.
Two figures fidget in separate silent circles
for minutes which feel like hours on this muzzle day.
Neither encounters the other. And

in the wine-washed fragrance of the transept
where her snatched, broken pearls
roll like her grief along cold stone, she
has a hug to spend. Sadly
unused at a funeral many distending years ago,
it burns a blue hole in the pocket where her soul is.
She cannot now clasp the dead, or those
whose comforts she spurned. But
someone will get it.
It must have somewhere to go.

Unseen a world away in the seeping churchyard,
somebody's arms kink hug-shaped,
a memory like unspooled fishing line; set
like the stare of one who is dying for you
to see them through a crowd.
She cannot now squeeze that lover or cling
to his long gone devotions and
someone else must have it.
It has to have somewhere to go.

Their silent circles now rustle. Footsteps.
St James's proximate worlds converge, two strangers
chance under creaking porch. With nowhere to go
they embrace.

We all have our own reasons.

Previously published in Confluence Magazine (Wordsmithery, Dec 2017)

PROSE BUSH

Should we weary of this limp walk,
one foot, one foot drug after the other?
Too many bruised
years, I roped you into this: shrinking
universe, bored with scattered silver. A penny
for black ragged thoughts that orbit
round, bound, wrung, spun
in whisky-on-the-rocks eyes. Give me
more. Open your door. Pour me
hot honey words tossed
in pearlescent cream. Yet
you rummage for them still
under dusty pews?
So much to say, mouth a black hole spewing stone-
cold ghosts, frayed, so very afraid... so shall we
skirt threatening suicide packed clouds,
then could we dance? Past drunk

dry apples you wouldn't harvest.
It all seemed so unreasonable. I saw you writhe
with her more slowly under those impotent
trees. There was no excuse really: she clipped
clean lead bones from us. Us!
born to sail sky script
clouds, pulse seed poems into black loam,
break
and crack
fingers of green shoot poets!
'No!

You may as well
burn them, spurn them,
shred them, behead them,

dead-head them,
tear them,
I can't bear them.
'Make mulch for the roses,' you cried.

Devoured by jade green critics who said the poems
were. . .
oh spite bites the quills that thrill
to compost bitter symphonies.

We dance our own dances
in our solar systems with dead suns. Long
to fling out my line, reel
you in to fill bent arms. Dream of spent
from hugging as we fire a new sun from blue
souls burning
holes in pockets. We became
strangers,
I see you from the graves, know
your reasons why you do that bee dance...

Fingers fumble clasp, your purse opens
my dud bud heart unfurls like a silly green lily.
I draw you in trapped shafts of treacle sunlight,
kiss-taste incense of your burning
gold hair again.

When you surrender me
poems, secrets, pearls and the key,
words drip rose furl lips, curl into
ragged poems at the frill, I breathe
in live poems
you scent of petals, bees and honey leas.
Our unforgiving suns have moved and scorched us
into an undiscovered universe.

POP!

Under the sun, black ragged,
limp walk on coerced earth.
Judge and jury bludgeon bully
intimidate the intimate, aggravate

desperate disparity
power imbalance, nothing but
the overwhelming might

just be no push
over and over, all might
just be dead delusion. Illusion soup.
Perception pop.

Pop!
Discerned means you
are disarmed. Parting
clouds could waggle dance
with me. Bee line to safe new

place. Listening in dense woods
where silverback gorillas scream smiling, dense
black bills adjusting their pristine sheens;

dropping naked acorns, fresh as peas
or bronzed with cracked lacquer,
onto a carpet of composted

bitterness. Join the feathered ape chorus;
macaque bird harmonies strung high. Limp onward
to the brow
unbeaten.

SOUP

Before the baby sun
had been hurled hot
into an unmade bed
of sky, before earth
was made,
compliant and lush,
we were dreaming
the world.
Cooking up ideas,
where nothing matters –
he coerced me, just once.
Asked for soup.
Just soup.
Nothing complex.
Just soup.

I want it without humans in.
Just a refreshing bowl
of soup for the soul.
Little things matter.
Soup matters.
Matter in the soup:
illusions and dreams,
hopes and art,
his dark materials,
to stir the soul.
And love. So much
love.
Love to be made.
There are many ways

to kill a man,
one could: harm
with charm,
cut,
drown,
crown,

disown,
dismember,
diss, hiss,
piss-take,
mistake,
disarm.
Cut down,
burn,
spurn,
tickle-taunt,
tar and feather,
strap with leather,
hail,
nail,

but remember this –
the easiest way,
by far the surest method
to kill a good man
once and for all,
is...

to slowly, ever so slowly...
keep him
alive.

You may have been lied to.
It was never blackbird
that Eden saw.
Crow was the first bird.
Black-green sheen,
never pristine
I wish he was mine.
I wish I was he
so I could stand
and look out before

Sea was made, before

I was given feathers and
say No No No,
keep it as soup,
just soup.
Scaled down
soup
without souls.

I read
Grief the Thing with Feathers.
It was much acclaimed.
I choked
on its screaming,
smiling, limping pages.
It bludgeoned me
to not understanding,
even though
it was about me,
bullied me to bed.
But I, Crow,
I am
in my own book.
Do not steal me
from my pages again.

She had Bees.
Furry bullets of fury
under no illusion who
their queen was.
Limping drones
to grind to bones –
but your honey
is so sweet...

The brow of the earth
is unbeaten,
unreasoned,
unseasoned,

its bowl unfilled,
miasma and mist.
Still soup.
Blank canvas.

So why birth the scorpion
or things with stings
and black barbed wings?

Come, my larder is full
of light materials.
Write. . .
new words
on my flesh,
with hands like doves.
They will become me.
There are no humans here
to hurt us.
Just us.
And these clean sheets

Refresh with peace,
go crow,
unblock the fountain.
Pens are flightier than swords,
plant mightier oaks
for the weary to rest
from earth's bitter kiss,
denounce the pressing hiss.
Part the silver
lacquered clouds
with your beak

and speak. Speak
living waters.

CLEAR

The woman reflected
in the train window looks
exactly like my musician friend, but
the real-life she does not.
I want to know if she
sounds like my friend too; maybe
her reflection sings but she is
silent? How can a woman not look like her reflection?

The other night I saw
a man shouting in the street. I knew
of his quiet and gentle soul, yet he jabbed
his finger in time with rapidly
coarsening words, his eyes wide with
indignation. Now honesty seemed to be his
second best policy, after anger – which reflects
very badly on him. How can a man not look like his
reflection?

There is a man who sings plush hymns
for pennies. "Oh what a beautiful
morning" he chants, through a traffic cone, even
on mornings which – like this one – are far
from beautiful. When I toss him a quid, and
even when I don't, he sounds cheerful but
his skin is distressed like his thin clothes.

It is clear
he can't sing like my friend but, as he sits
with his back against diamond pixels of opulent Halifax
glass,
I can only wonder whether he
looks like his reflection.

I see them all from their graves.

TWO FOLD SOULS

After January slushed harsh snows, flushed frosts,
when sky-shy sun showed her lush lemon face,
when I dropped the perfect purl poem, I lost
myself twice over
and did not know where I might be. In my search
in a clearing of silver birch I saw
mighty men, gods even, besides themselves, crying
over rivers amongst narcissi that sheared
their darling faces. The early-bloomed, the doomed,
the human and the inhumane walk
the streets of London, Rochester, the countryside.

The watchmen waited, hated, slew me, threw me
in the two-tone water wild: some parts,
black as hearts, the woes in my belly
sloe sank me. If they had a mind to,
to rent me open, all the men I loved
would have crawled out shaking
my still hot blood off their hands. I am
half girl, half verse but who will trace
my two mother tongues on my skin?

It is a grave thing to split
the soul in two,
to consider which part of you will just not...

lie flat. Like a crumpled poem.

Do men know the soft syllables I would sing to shake
them. The gentle 'o' sung in mornings. How half of me
would kiss him silver.
Stars, lacquer cracked, are swallowed whole by black

masses in a binary system and only the main points
flung back to be forced home
with sharp fingers. Slack from our graves
we are drug, the purple night
shade is drawn. The silver lies hammered
and quartered. We all see a different face
slung back, the ebb and flow of tired tides.

Oh come to me with the sheaf
of transparent honesty lying in the crook
of warrior arms. I stitched new
moons on your shirts but the button holes
contracted, shrank. To come or to go
I did not know..

It is a grave thing to split another's soul
in two to consider which part of you will just not do..

for me.
You cut sweet hearts
with a switch blade. Through the oven door I saw myself
softly rising. Your heart was goldening, so I turned,
slipped buttery words from fool fingers: skewered words,

knifed words, pierced parts,
they burned...

My soul, I ask you why the inside of a technicolour
dream
coat is turned grey,
and the under-bellies of rare blue kittens
are not always white.
Young yielding acorns fall green with no faerie cap,

show no signs of mighty oakiness. We see

through smoked glass – darkly, I see
these things: we are all
broken...

puppets, strung wrong, taut strings,
taught wrong songs, wrong things.
Here lie the hungry men, hung with no soup,
slung stars singing for supper, gin-soaked
ghosts writhing
in pane of opulent glass. I wonder
if I can be seen. Are smiles honestly just
a line upon a face, am I my own
reflection or the sum of your thoughts, I wonder
can anyone hear my soaring music from across the road
of me?

It is a grave thing to split the soul in two
to consider which part of you will rot...

in libraries, streets and trains,
half of me knows this.
The same Lot awaits every man, all-sorts,
those plush with plenty, those with not
a lot, or those poor souls without even a plot
or a pillow, we all become that salt.
Of the Earth – both the hiss and kiss
lay lusciously in the grave. Even the fair
fall to the grassing green in the dark drifting
bliss of chocolate arms.

I know this: windows may lie, hearts always do
but you will see yourself, even two of you perfectly,

exquisitely formed
in the eyes of somebody who
loves you.

A rounded hall, with soft suede walls,
mirrors and disco balls casting
myriad me.
So many places to hang
a creased soul.
He folded mine twice
and pocketed me away.

My poem is lost forever.
But I am ten thousand women with a million
poems if I believe
hard enough. I will...

awaken a new angel and pact grey mournings away,
I will sing songs ripe and full as an orange.
I walked strange
streets, heard bees hum, drum a requiem: some torn,
sworn
to butterflies,
the honey jarred.

When unfolded and the two halves separated,
even those pinned and mounted had perfectly
symmetrical wings
and velvet eyes stitched to their wings for 'I's to fall
into. The bees, their stings
had torn them inside
out, the shade so terrible,
that a good man should never see.

But my fate is sealed

into my seasoned skin like those shameless
women of lore who hid slick oiled
seal cloaks behind rocks
on the shell-shocked shore to live
seamlessly amongst men, baking and sewing
and birthing and salting meat whilst aching
with silvery stories of the sea in their bellies.

SLACKEN

Air is liquid,   loose
change, untied wild weather or
knot in stomach loosed by its casual hands;
sighs wide open, eyes the
back of sky's head-space;
Monday breathes gorgeous and loads
at a snail's pace, hoisted
high on sufficient air to fill November.

Tension's knotwear, tight as night,
tumbles – all love and misery's mute grumble –
tangled garments in the drum,
treacle-brushed and sloshed by blasé
coils in gentlest unfurl-pool;
reposed sleeves and legs   limp,
turning like conductors' hands in
weightless figure eights

Tension's fist lets go, crazy
moves freely drenched gin
bubbles, tonic hisses kissed
with liquid smoke. Living
water, living well. Unpicked storm clasp,
latch and zipper –   relax.
Air hushed and slate lushed hard;
fluidity's coquettish breezes
salvage savage primate minds.

Tension's physics fall apart
in molten safety. Air is sloth blood
orange, amber columns and sloe soup;
idle hands slid between worry-buttons;

Motion quickness well
stagnated. White knuckles, mulch for
silvered roses.　　　　Slackened –
curled-up tongues, now princely bracken
fronds. Unfold. Breathe.
Air's dark drifting bliss: fluid, free
to fill worlds and winters.

TO FALL: IN LOVE

Cider kissed air decides, pleads: reap, gather
me before I spoil. Blue opened sky-eyes wide,
bright Spring had uncoiled quickly, hurtling bold
into Summer, who, now she is old, is young
enough again to love, flew fast forward, flush
in her sprigged dress. Tarnished gold-greened, slow
slipped her condemned
shoulder, spooled, floored, hemmed red
replete at her sweet feet. Scrumped fruits are juiciest
just before the sherbet sharp sun
burst, trees bested with slick crimson vest already
flagrantly fruited and spored. Berry red cape hangs
limp from tired tree's fork, fresh flesh quick
rots to heady fizzing perfume in ferny beds,
stirs bled birds who fled the dead

to seek new Summers now. Dread
white wolves slow slunk on their blue bellies full
of sob-sorry stones. 'There are too many odes
to autumn, mine will never sail script skies.'
Summer cried, wanted someone...someone
gold enough to sing 'you are my portion.' But
the wild wanton woods stayed silent: nor did
the leave-ings whisper soft nor scrolled her name

but hissed 'did Fall come before the scarlet apple
fell?' Sky sigh-says it is a time for plenty, she is a lie
plus twenty and she wants, waits, wants...
waits   for nothing...
Love is longed for, summer-songed for.
When tongues loosened, birds swagged, woods rolled
out blush red carpet, the trees were strolling loose

limbed: uncurled fists that once imprisoned buds,
longed for love, that seasoned kiss.
Apples grounded, flawed, pawed, pock marked and
scored. Velvet plush, cream crush mushrooms bloomed
and rounded, smell of soil and mist, stirring
silken slump soup underfoot. Plump squash swell well,
tree skirts fall, drip-drop plum amethysts. She is old,
she is young enough for love...
to shine.   Conquer

love before sleep, before the golden wheat is shamed
and shorn, mill her heart to wild flours that once
blue-filled full the whole field. Cidered wasps
are too exhausted
for war. . . flies bottling out, everything
has its time, even the skeleton leaves. When I am sold
old
again, this is the season that will be missed: its apple
mulch
in the lichen, the mellow fruit-fullness, I think
this artful, heart-full Autumn will be
my worn Summer that was spent,
wasted,   tense

is past. Winter will march in, welcome with her white
army to dredge, drift and sift.
In the glorious deaths, a purity, a whipped, stripped
un-torn sworn truth. No sealed lairs to conceal
limpet cloaks clung to salt rocks. Warm white-washed
wind's gentle assaults will court: bow and lift, spin
soft strung spun souls, hung,
to dry, hoisted high. Swung loose from brilliant
bone clean boughs, they know

they have set dandelion clocks back.

Then Spring will tumble in on slack reigns
with days nailed in place, running at snail's pace.

WOLF

Fear is the Dread
Wolf
stalking with black stoop
to conquer sleep. ECHO, echo, echo...
belly slunk blue and snuck through
his gut drags the blackened blizzard
remains. With owls he shouts smoke
signals in darkness.

Fear is the Dread
Wolf
choking on the
rounded smell of soil and mist
opportunities butchered.
Fangs so close bauble window
gleams your eye, with howls
of distemper wind in half-light.

Fear is the Dread
Wolf
in sheep's winter coat. Elongated,
barren white atomic bombs can't reach
to stain. Forget to breathe: the air
is colic; albino spiders; terror tunnel.
Too much space dazzles blind and
timorous ECHO, echo, echo...

As long as there's a sun I'll curl
with rabid beasts in driving snow, warm
in their sleek pulses; quarry for their danger den
blanketed in peril; rather this than menace
by echoes. Because blunt wind knows, as

I know that Fear
is the real Dread
Wolf.

DANCING WITH WOLVES IN MY EYES

Who stole my sun? Put her back now and
we will say no more about it. Shadows loom
in crooked places. Where you were cast rod straight
at noon, now I see your long shadow shyly limp
the valley at two. It's a different sky to when

we rolled in snowy fields. Now the clement sun
carves a tilt, hangs
lower and paler in the sky. A timid Sunday,
we lope above cliff faces, brighter
than lithium, charged, waiting

for night. But... for now
sun glows huge,
bubble bright. Peeks a stark, clawing tree
as we turn gently into our quiet lanes,
sets hands ablaze before even the dark

sleeps. Should you stop turning
as night sloe, slow, slow dances, when
the Shades of Fear rear, I will remember
the clean sharp whistle power of snow-
falling –

into atomic eyes and seeing the you reflected
in my eyes reflected back in yours
and I can pinch out
the white flame. Take your breath away.
Dishes don't run away with spoons

and it is no laughing matter.
Small dogs can cast huge shadows
when the simmering sun rages, rages,
                                        You lost yourself twice
over
and I didn't know where you may be.

Ages pelt past, memories trapped
in warm blankets cloaking fear stained
years, the howl of days, dreams
pawed at the corners. 6000 days,
life in the cold, measured in aching

heartbeats.
Counting is what makes us human.
They say it takes four minutes.
The peril of living. Any man is damned
if he doesn't.

Turn back and see the curve
of your long limbs in soft silver
and remember them
one last time as gold atoms danced sly
upon you amongst snow tip blades.

When lunacy wanes will I remember
those chemical romances and dances
burnt hard against the moon,
sad stars doing their best
to spurn their black, and not look.

When the steel spade axes the bridled white
earth, I will watch you fetch
the ripe sun. Yes, the sky has changed
and I must change too. It waits
for no man.

It is Time he said.
One wore a grey cloak and the other
shone
                                        as they drifted away
below dazzling horizons
and he stood: the only man in the world.

THEN

There
he stood,
then. Then.
The only man on Earth: crisp
white-shirted, besmirked, straw-hatted,
yearning from a lamppost, jaunty angling for special
sunny sentences to be released from behind barred
windows.

No thicker than breath, yet
windows choose which world
you sing to. Open it up,
then. One call, one man,
one word, one action. And
then.

Here
he stands
now. Counting
quiet lanes in the mind
despite the Neal Street bustle and six
thousand vivid tastes measured by Seven Dials
now. His scarlet song smiles solo, the only man on
earth.

Every angst now blunted. Silence
now well-fitting as a mended shoe.
Memories curl in warmed blankets.
Sunday all day back then. Only man
on earth seeking lasting last hug.
Now.

MATCH

If I didn't wear my red shoes I'd float
away from here to happily ever after.
I wore my world thin. With needing love
and needling needs, I clasped passion
loosely around me but it never fit. Mostly
said I was not cold, did not need much
warmth, too casual, tight or didn't match.
The best fit, unappreciated, I left it loose
thrown in a heap on the bedroom floor.

I will never forget, once upon a time, a face
in a white coat shouting, you cannot live
in your own skin can you? But, oh I made
such soft skin, pliant bones and a tiny dress
the only dress ever worn, blood-berry red,
and my basket is still full of treachery cake.

I knit a thousand worlds, in one I heard
a boy cry – for the only love that will lull
to sleep, although the limp skin worn out
and limbs hung loose, the straw fallen
to the ends, still, only this one would do.

I saw a lone man singing by a lamp-post
and a rabbit swinging limp over a fence
He had been there seven weeks   or a thousand
years:
wet, sodden, down trodden, and needing
love, I took him home. My son pleaded
give him a new hat and new un-tired skin
and new fat filling. Wept four-year-old pain
when I told him if he was made new
he would be a different creature. We lay
the wet thing between us, loved him dry,
loved him all the more for being broken.

I don't want my feet under this table.
Where a small boy cries why doesn't
my daddy come home like other daddies do.
I want love that fits like a second skin.
A thousand windows – I closed them all.
The ones that are open – I do not want those
songs. The one song I want: that heart
cannot read the words, strung out
to dry like wet bunting on rusting railings,
the treasons why I loved him forgotten.

Like the little match girl I can only dream now
of warming my fingers at someone else's fires.
I leave my red shoes on the window sill:
the fire will take them, take us all eventually
into its world of pictures.

I wonder what words were breathed
into the first man
to make him come alive.

I have taken my fill from fountains
and am still empty, food will never sustain,
need wine, milk and honey tongue tipped
cake made of words, saliva syllables, toothsome
tercets, tongue twisters:

my lips are a purse of prose
there is only one way to a man's heart.

It takes a secret combination of letters to unlock
unbutton my seems with lines, words,
echoing off cold damp walls in
this house I grew up in.

I see myself floating upwards
from that sill, the red shoes:
the fire has not licked them yet.
So high up, so very far away, it may never reach.
They hold me back, and my blue taut skin…

These are my wrung out love
letters drying in the wind.
These are mine.
This is my heart smelted in two,
fierce flames pirouetting.
Sometimes I dream, sometimes I stay the same.
There are not many of us left now –
after so many empty midnights –
that seek love in crevices and cracks of daylight
in love-burnt eyes that cannot see.

The writing is on the wall:
the dark matters of my heart – I do not know
how to sway it.

Words branding the tip of the tongue,
about to fall off the precipice
just at the sharp edge of making the cut.
Snow sizzling on scarlet fire.
Fire, fire on the lips felt finger tips,
scribing hot testaments on broken sleeping tablets.
The wry kiss at the corner of the mouth that
the flames strive to prise open –
I think I will always wonder what genius tastes like.

Smoked out of my hiding, I am ready
for the flames to take me,
I shrug off my skin.
This is me, my fortune, my fate –

looking through festive windows
undressed, their red velvet parted
and I dream...

I dream of picking the last
juicy morsels from the carcass
before our bones,
all of our bones are thrown
to the fire.

COLOUR-MATCH

Tomorrow was so long ago when we woke to
old Grey swatch; a hundred hues and we
couldn't even dream in Rain Cloud now; when
the sun rose like a sunset; when
a boar's head inclined, its Night Smoke
eye winking worlds of pictures; when
a slow, slow Charcoal hearse bowed its backing
and Slate Grey sleeves were squeezed solid; when
half-remembered people left it loose and –
gathered here, in sure and certain – we hugged
the nervy land as Mist Cloud eyes warmed us
through, lulled to sleep as hasty day wore thin.

Spirits were Weathered Lead but, respects paid
and loves outed, we knew we were blessed and dressed

to live again, only craved life worth the bother.
He'd want us to and soon we'd have our glorious
routines:
crooning nature's language, heaving burly boots
somehow jaunty through winter's Silvered Sludge;
Onyx velvet collar turned up like the postcard;
Tales of reservoirs and half-crown snowflakes –
bleached swans gliding the ten pale acres
between a white land and a whiter sky.

Never did quite conquer summers but, in the chill,
as Pewter Shadow leaves leave shadows,
we've been imparted to: there's no such thing as colour
blind
to those that pound the diverse coloured stones with spit
and, with a match, adorn the ancient pavement.
Sixty shades at number twenty five.

AULD LANG SYNE

We take our brushes with death
and paint each other
as monsters.

Deep down I know –
we are glorious,
the beautiful ones.
When bugs crawl
where our hearts were –

they have eaten our names,
consumed our banners.

The proud moments:
every monster fed at a warm breast once.

Mother says he knows
his colours now –

lips are red.
And blue aconite takes out the heart...

I want you to know mine.
Are they ever true?

Love lies between us
as always.
Remorse flung to roadsides,
it will take root, amongst fading
forget-me-nots.

When I tried to save
you from the raging
                fire,
I was no match for myself.
I should have worn
the sensible blue shoes.

In absolute death throes I turned
to kill you.

Is sorrow a colour you can stomach?
Will you take it neat
from my tongue? Love seeks
not its own.

Buildings lie in dust, cities ruined,
you said you had no use for new.
Midnight –
you shot 18 pieces of silver from the sky.
But I didn't believe in the drowning.

I dug it all up,
examining the gleaned bones of it,
connected the ankle to the thigh bone
and the heart to the bile duct.

Three unwise men: I buried them.
I wanted
to put the old back
in its place.
They made me –
alive.

The youngest one: I had to dig the deepest
grave – should I pull him out to kiss

behind city stones where wild roses grew,
his vanilla head.

Smashed watch-men at the gates.
They should be sacked due to their unreliability.
They tied up Janus, rolled him in the mud,
dismissed the murders, burials and exhumations as
good-natured fun.

What if they rise and kill me?

Lips plump and pink,
all are just a slightly different shade of delicious,
and all beauty must
die.

Quickly – the most beautiful, their dye bleeds the lines,
these ones were harder to hold,
red ribbon soft slips

hands. He has big hands. Bigger than I
remember. It took him 5 years
to resurrect, some do take longer... He said
he had seen me from the side-lines
moving mighty mountains and sometimes falling

down, I said falling is my speciality.
He said, No darling-rising up is...
Before I killed him, did I tell him I loved him?

Bury, keep, bury keep, bury,
I do not know what will become of us all.
What colour is your fire? I cannot bear to cleave
red and orange, touch cold blue at the base,
insipid soft yellow that can barely lick.

Is there any meat left on our carcass?

Less good is love when it paints everything black.
Give me the indigo velvet of twelve again,
powdery hands tucking in the corners of my soul,
a rest in a silk pocket.

Being dead is the only way to be alive.
There is only one way to kill a man, love
till you drain
all his colour till he is puce and sick
of you.

I want hope to be fizzy on the tongue,
standing tall like the bravest first silly daffodil.

Do loving arms reach this far,
to that place before
the world was made, before I birthed black
things with wings and hideous
stings?

I can't even contain myself...
This box will not contain me,
my lines fuzzy and blurred.

Knowing we can be monsters keeps us safe.
I turned because the moon was not full yet –
it still had things to devour...

This is my heart smelted in two – this is
my final love letter.
Burying someone alive is hard.
Others made me do it.
I will sit on my hands.

I will beg to dig you up
dress you in white.

Till I kill love for good
I have no shame –
full – I am naked.

I wear it well –
snake skin green shed at my feet.

Am I strawberry, fig, blueberry or sloe?
Am I raspberry eaten after October's kiss
when they say Lucifer breathed
Death upon them?
What fruit? what colour?
Or do you not much care?
It is hard to describe me now.
Am I royal purple or edging toward the eternal
black?

Hands turn to an indignant midnight,
my red dress folds to grey rags,
gold chariot squashed, the rifle
cracks, and hope longs
to lie on the first page and hear
your mirth...

fall in time with long strides.
There is no need
for shoes in the grave
I surrender my scarlet.

When I first beheld you I dressed
you in gold before grey –
the final shroud too heavy to bear.

Don't return the crown I bestowed –
you can be a king forever...

Remember the shape of me please.
It all matters so much in the dark.

The only picture I see in these
flames is your face –
sadness is the colour of
these empty sheets.

To the wind, I am just lines now
furrowed in the earth.
My colours have bled out of me.

I know you won't let me warm my hands now.
Remembering we can be monsters is what will keep us
safe.

I need to return to the Motherlands.

Through the oven door,
I see myself
creamy and soft
slowly
rising.

Is that white linen laid out for me?

Poems by Matt Chamberlain

Many little midnights
Losing touch
Embrace
Pop!
Clear
Slacken
Wolf
Then
Colour-match

Poems by Angela Dye

Feeling blue
Matters of the heart
Prose bush
Soup
Two fold souls
To fall: in love
Dancing with wolves in my eyes
Match
Auld Lang Syne

ABOUT THE AUTHORS

Angela Dye is a poet, novelist, script-writer, teacher, part-time journalist and full-time artistic dynamo, published in various anthologies and magazines. She is assistant editor for Confluence magazine, mentor on the Wordsmithery writer development programme, founder of Kent's 'Wanted: Dead or Alive' poetry events and curator of community festivals. She runs writing workshops in Faversham and regularly reads her own work at venues around Kent. She currently has three other poetry books in development.

Matt Chamberlain has previously published five poetry collections (one a collaboration with Spreken) and featured in various magazines, journals and anthologies. He is a three time winner of the international Poetry Pulse competition and, more locally, he has held both the H. E. Doust and Alice E. Wright trophies for spoken performance. His work has featured on CD, radio and film. He regularly performs at a range of live performance events, from open mic nights to literary events, festivals to charity fundraisers. He was the first festival laureate for the Vicar's Picnic music festival.